Table of Contents

Introduction 5

Chapter 1: What is Anxiety 9

Chapter 2: The Effects of Anxiety 11

Chapter 3: Simple Strategies for Overcoming Anxiety 14

Chapter 4: Physical Methods for Combating Worry and Anxiety 22

    Diet 23

    Exercise 30

    Sleep 34

    Relaxation Techniques 40

Chapter 5: Perspective 44

Chapter 6: Meditation 52

Chapter 7: Mindfulness 61

Chapter 8: Managing Anxiety at Work and Other Specific Locations 71

Chapter 9: Conclusion 76

"Worry a little bit every day and in a lifetime you will lose a couple of years. If something is wrong, fix it if you can. But train yourself not to worry. Worry never fixes anything."

- Mary Hemingway

Introduction

Do you worry a lot? Many people operate under the fallacy that worrying is productive. **However, our worries have no impact on the rest of the world.** No one has ever worried away bad weather or a faulty automobile transmission. As much as we like to think that all the time and energy we put into worrying is helpful, it's not.

Anxiety is a major cause of many emotional and physical ailments. Anxiety and worry are a major cause of unhappiness and poor health. Anxiety is also incredibly common.

Everyone worries from time to time.

Thankfully, anxiety and worry are under our control. You can stop worrying whenever you truly decide to put an end to it.

Here's what we're covering in this book:

Chapter 1: What is Anxiety? It's important to understand what anxiety is and isn't if you're going to address its presence in your life.

Chapter 2: The Effects of Anxiety. Anxiety causes more harm than just that queasy feeling in your stomach. There are serious emotional, physical, and life satisfaction implications, too.

Chapter 3: Simple Strategies for Overcoming Anxiety. Sometimes simple strategies are enough. These quick and easy techniques will take the edge off the worry and anxiety in your life.

Chapter 4: Physical Methods for Combating Worry and Anxiety. Sleep, diet, exercise, and relaxation techniques can reduce the baseline level of stress in your life and leave you more capable of dealing with any stress that remains.

Chapter 5: Perspective. Your view of life and the world impacts what causes worry and anxiety. With a new perspective, you can eliminate many of the most common causes of anxiety and worry.

ALL RIGHTS RESERVED. No part of this report may be modified or altered in any form whatsoever, electronic, or mechanical, including photocopying, recording, or by any informational storage or retrieval system without express written, dated and signed permission from the author.

AFFILIATE DISCLAIMER. The short, direct, non-legal version is this: Some of the links in this report may be affiliate links which means that I earn money if you choose to buy from that vendor at some point in the near future. I do not choose which products and services to promote based upon which pay me the most, I choose based upon my decision of which I would recommend to a dear friend. You will never pay more for an item by clicking through my affiliate link, and, in fact, may pay less since I negotiate special offers for my readers that are not available elsewhere.

DISCLAIMER AND/OR LEGAL NOTICES: The information presented herein represents the view of the author as of the date of publication. Because of the rate with which conditions change, the author reserves the right to alter and update his opinion based on the new conditions. The report is for informational purposes only.

While every attempt has been made to verify the information provided in this report, neither the author nor his affiliates/partners assume any responsibility for errors, inaccuracies or omissions. Any slights of people or organizations are unintentional. If advice concerning legal or related matters is needed, the services of a fully qualified professional should be sought. This report is not intended for use as a source of legal or accounting advice. You should be aware of any laws which govern business transactions or other business practices in your country and state. Any reference to any person or business whether living or dead is purely coincidental.

Copyright © 2021

Text & Illustrations © 2021, 2023 by Lorne S. Wellington

All rights reserved. This book or any portion thereof may not be reproduced or used in any manner whatsoever without the express written permission of the publisher, except for the use of brief quotations in a book review.

Cover Art Design: Lorne S. Wellington

ISBN: 979-8-9903832-0-3 Paperback

ISBN: 979-8-9903832-1-0 Kindle

ISBN: 979-8-9903832-2-7 Audio

Trademark information Big World Publishing, Los Angeles, CA. Cataloguing in Publication Data available upon request from Library and Archives United States of America.

Printed in United States of America

Chapter 6: Meditation. The ancient practice of meditation has seen a strong revival in recent years. It's not complicated but requires practice. It's more beneficial than you think.

Chapter 7: Mindfulness. Mindfulness is a close relative of meditation. Both boost each other.

Chapter 8: Managing Anxiety at Work and Other Specific Locations. You know the techniques, but can you apply them outside the comfort of your home?

Chapter 9: Conclusion. What's next? Further steps you can take to reduce your anxiety.

"Worry is a thin stream of fear trickling through the mind. If encouraged, it cuts a channel into which all other thoughts are drained."

- Arthur Somers Roche

Chapter 1: What is Anxiety

According to the dictionary, anxiety is a feeling of worry, nervousness, or unease, typically about an imminent event or something with an uncertain outcome. It's your body's reaction to stress.

Everyone knows what anxiety feels like. It's that feeling in the pit of your stomach on the first day of school. It's also the feeling you get when you know you have to give a speech in an hour.

We can think of anxiety as an overall state combining fear, worry, and uncertainty. It's physical and emotional. It's often a reaction to something that hasn't happened yet and may never happen. It's largely anticipatory.

While anxiety is most often focused on a particular event, it is possible to have anxiety in a more general sense. These are often classified as anxiety disorders.

"Worrying about it takes precious time and attention away from your priorities and increases your feelings of dissatisfaction about life."

- Christina Winsey-Rudd

Chapter 2: The Effects of Anxiety

Anxiety is hard on your mind and body. While anxiety is occasionally a good thing when it saves your life or prevents you from doing something overly risky, it causes more harm than good in most cases.

Chronic anxiety can cause a host of physical and emotional symptoms, including:

- Fatigue
- Rapid heart rate
- High blood pressure
- Inability to concentrate
- Hyperventilation
- Insomnia
- Shortness of breath
- Headaches
- Dizziness
- Panic attacks

- Anxiety disorders
- Sweating

Long-term risks include:

- Immune system suppression. This can lead to a variety of illnesses from the common cold, to the flu, or even cancer.
- Digestive disorders
- Heart disease

Anxiety has a wide variety of negative effects on the mind and body. Anxiety also limits your life in many ways. It can stifle your career and social life. It also limits your enjoyment.

Think about how much different your life would look if you never worried. This might seem like a silly idea, but it's not. You might have to grow older, but there's no rule that says you have to be anxious.

"There is only one way to happiness and that is to cease worrying about things which are beyond the power of our will."

- Epictetus

Chapter 3: Simple Strategies for Overcoming Anxiety

There are many ways to approach anxiety. **The simplest methods are also the best.** While we'll explore more involved ways to ease anxiety, try giving a few simple methods a chance. You might get the relief you need without a lot effort.

Use these strategies to worry less:

1. **Ask yourself what you can do about it.** There are many worries that are beyond your ability to influence. If you can do something about your concern, by all means, do it. However, many of our worrisome situations can't be solved. A few examples include:

    o   Health issues of a family member

- The weather for the family reunion on Saturday
- Whether or not you'll get that promotion or raise on Monday
- Whether or not someone likes you
- Whether or not your child had a good day at school today
- Politics
- Your sports team's performance
- The list is endless. You have less influence on your environment than you think. Remind yourself that worrying about these types of items is pointless.

2. **Get more rest.** A lack of sleep only makes anxiety issues worse. Your body produces many of the same chemicals while fatigued as it does when you're stressed. The conditions are very similar.

    - **An extra hour of sleep each night can make a big difference.** A nap can be helpful, too.

3. **Find something else to do.** If worry and anxiety are getting the best of you, try distracting yourself. You might think, "That's not going to solve anything." True, but neither is worrying. You may as well enjoy yourself as much as possible in the meantime.

4. **Adopt powerful body language.** Strong, powerful body language can change your mood and attitude. Try standing like a powerful person that has control over his life.

    - Head up
    - Stand or sit up straight
    - Chest out
    - Slight smile
    - Take up space
    - Have a strong handshake
    - Relaxed
    - Good eye contact
    - Watch a few movies with powerful, confident characters and notice how they stand and move

5. **Laugh.** You have a couple of memories or stories that always make you laugh when you think about them or share them. Have these memories ready to go at a moment's notice.

    - Who is the funniest person you know? Spend more time with them when you're feeling stressed.
    - What tv shows or movies always make you laugh? Do you have access to them? Are there any YouTube videos you find funny? Save them them so you have access to them at any time.
    - Who are your favorite comedians?

6. **Limit your worrying to a set amount of time.** Does worrying make you feel a little better? Okay, worry away. But, you can only worry for 30 minutes! Plan your worrying time in advance. Put it on your calendar and really work up to it. Set a timer and have at it.

- Ensure that you don't worry until your designated time. If you start worrying before, catch yourself and say, "I'll worry tomorrow at 5PM. It's on my calendar!"

7. **Avoid assumptions.** Many of our problems, fears, and worries are the result of assumptions. Why assume that things are going to go poorly? Why not just assume things will go well? Neither will affect the outcome, but you'll enjoy your life more if you have positive expectations.

    - Assumptions can also cause anxiety in other ways. We assume that someone doesn't like us. Or we assume that we'll never find a better job. We assume that nothing we try will work, so why try at all?

    - Rather than make assumptions, why not give yourself a chance and see what actually happens?

8. **Be willing to say no.** Worry, stress, and anxiety are the common result of an inability to refuse requests. We over promise and over commit. We often even commit to doing things that violate our values and personal priorities.

    o When you can say no, you're setting boundaries that protect your time, energy, and sanity. Be honest and tell people that you don't have the time.

9. **Make a plan for the worst.** It can be helpful to imagine the worst possible outcome and prepare for it.

    o The worst possible outcome likely won't happen, but if you have a plan to deal with it, you can relax. You're already covered.

10. **Accept that worry is just an uncomfortable feeling in your body.** Like all emotions, anxiety and worry are physical sensations that you

experience. You don't have to change your life plans or avoid certain activities because you have a mosquito bite on your arm. You wouldn't allow that to stop you from doing anything.

- **You can choose to just allow your anxiety to exist and move forward anyway.**

While meditation, mindfulness training, and changing your view of the world are powerful techniques, a few, quick simple solutions might be enough to take the edge off your excessive worrying. **Never discount simple techniques without giving them a trial run.** You could save yourself a lot of time.

'He is rich who owns the day, and no one owns the day who allows it to be invaded with fret and anxiety."

- Ralph Waldo Emerson

Chapter 4: Physical Methods for Combating Worry and Anxiety

There are two general approaches to dealing with worry and anxiety: A physical approach and a psychological approach. **Both are worth investigating.** Perhaps one approach will be enough to provide the relief you desire. In most cases, using both will bring the best results.

Physical methods are mostly lifestyle changes. These changes are also beneficial to your overall health and wellbeing. It won't just be your anxious mind that benefits.

There are many physical benefits as well.

Diet

This might be more specific for you than just eating your veggies and avoiding ice cream. There are people that have been able to stop taking anxiety medication just by dropping gluten from their diet. You can't be sure what the best diet is for you until you experiment. Your diet has a huge impact on your physical and mental health.

Some likely culprits that can contribute to anxiety or general discomfort include:

- Dairy
- Gluten
- Processed meats, such as bacon and sausage
- Artificial colors and flavorings
- Caffeine
- Nuts
- Even egg whites cause a rapid heart rate in some people

Some people have no problems with these foods, while others have problems with all of them. It's likely there is at least one item on this list that negatively affects you.

"The truth is that there is no actual stress or anxiety in the world; it's your thoughts that create these false beliefs. You can't package stress, touch it, or see it. There are only people engaged in stressful thinking."

- Wayne Dyer

Build a healthy diet just for you from scratch:

1. **Start with an extremely healthy diet.** Start with the healthiest diet you can stand for a few days. You probably won't have to maintain this diet for long, but you could! Here's a list of foods you can eat:

   - Any fruit, vegetable, legume, or organic meat

   - Water

   - That's it. In case you're wondering, legumes are beans, lentils, peas, and peanuts. But skip the peanuts.

2. **Eat this way for a week.** No cheating allowed. After a week, notice how you feel. If you feel much better, you should be very excited! If you feel the same, your old diet probably isn't causing you any stress or anxiety.

3. **Start adding back in the foods you think you can't live without.** Each

morning, you're going to test one food with the following procedure.

- Sit quietly for a minute with the food in front of you. Rate how you feel physically and psychologically on a scale of 1 to 10.

- Take your pulse. If you have a blood pressure monitor, you can use that, too. Record your pulse.

- Eat the food slowly with a small glass of water. Avoid any other foods at this time. This should be the first thing you've eaten for the day. Only test one food each day.

- After finishing the food, take your pulse again. If it has risen more than 10 beats from your starting measurement, that food may be causing it.

- Rate how you feel again. If you feel worse, stay away from that food. If you feel the same, you can continue eating it.

4. **Over time, you can test every food that appeals to you.** Remember to check any sauces and salad dressings that you like to eat. These are often an issue for many people. Beverages, too!

Diet matters. **Most people vastly underestimate the impact diet has on their physical and emotional health.** Consider that you're putting food into your body. It's then broken down and travels through your bloodstream. Of course, the food you eat is going to have a huge effect on how you feel.

In some cases, this one item can be enough to change your life dramatically. Give this strategy a fair chance.

"I think that fear comes about when there's things in the world that we want to change, things we're scared or angry about, and we can't change them, and so we become fearful; we develop anxiety."

- Michael Franti

Exercise

You already know that exercise is good for you. But exercise is easy to put off to another day. **You might feel that you're too stressed or busy for exercise, but exercise might be exactly what you need to reduce your stress.** Exercise can be a simple way to reduce anxiety and make you more worry- resistant.

Exercise provides stress-defeating benefits, including:

1. **Exercise destroys many of the chemicals your body releases when you're stressed.** You're removing part of the cause for your stressed feelings when you exercise.

2. **Exercise releases endorphins.** These neurotransmitters make you feel good. Any vigorous exercise can release endorphins. They're strong enough to create an addiction to exercise.

3. **It focuses your mind on something other than your worries.** When you have a tennis ball flying at you at 80 miles per hour, your mind is focused on the game. You're not worrying about your unpaid parking tickets or the fact that your boss yelled at you.

    - Moving your body is a great way to make your mind more focused on the present moment.

    - Even going for a leisurely walk can be beneficial. This, along with controlling your body, can distract your mind from your challenges.

4. **Find exercise that you love.** It's easier to exercise when you enjoy it. Find something you love to do and build it into your schedule.

How much exercise do you need to feel better? Experiment and determine the amount that works best for you. Some people do quite well with short 10-minute walks. Others need to really work up a sweat. Stay within your current capabilities but give both styles of exercise a try and find what works for you.

"Amusement is appealing because
we don't have to think; it spares us the fear
and anxiety that might otherwise
prey on our thoughts."

- John Ortberg

Sleep

You're busy, so you might think you don't have time to get more sleep. **But, it's important to remember that sleep is good for your health.** A lack of sleep can be a significant source of physical stress. Then you feel awful physically which leads to feeling awful emotionally.

Sleep is one of the best ways to keep anxiety and worry away from your doorstep:

1. **It's about quality and quantity.** The magic number from numerous studies is seven hours of sleep. You might think you only need six hours but give seven a chance and notice how you feel.

    - But not all hours of sleep are created equal. If you toss and turn all night, ten hours might be insufficient.

2. **Create a good sleeping environment.** You wouldn't choose to sleep on a

concrete driveway in the middle of a 90-degree day. Sleeping in a hot room on an old, squishy, lumpy mattress isn't ideal either.

- Dark and quiet is ideal for most people.
- Find the right mattress and pillow.
- Find your ideal temperature. Experiment.
- Avoid using the bedroom for anything other than sleep and sex.
- Get rid of the TV.
- No working in the bedroom!
- Keep your cell phone away from the immediate area.

3. **Set a regular sleep schedule.** College students might be able to get away with constantly changing sleep schedules, but those days are over. Do everything you can to stick to a regular schedule.

4. **Nap, but be careful.** A regular nap can be a great way to get more sleep. Experiment with the right length of time. Naps that are too long can leave you feeling groggy and disoriented.

    - Occasional napping can potentially be a good thing. If you're making up for missed sleep, the occasional nap can be useful. But, occasional napping can also throw off your sleep routine. A nap in the afternoon might make it hard to fall asleep at night.

5. **Use light to your advantage.** You'll wake up more readily in the morning if you expose yourself to sunlight in the morning. There are even artificial lights that mimic the sunlight you can use in the winter.

    - **Limit your exposure to bright electronic screens in the evening.** Too much light keeps your brain too active and awake.

6. **Avoid TV at night.** Between the bright screen and the stimulating content, watching television can make it harder to sleep at night. Listening to music or to a book on tape can be better options if sleep is a priority.

7. **Exercise can help you sleep.** Avoid exercising within four hours of your bedtime if possible. Some people sleep quite well shortly after exercising. You can't be sure how you'll respond without experimenting.

    o Exercising too hard or for too long can have a negative impact on sleep. In fact, one of the signs of overtraining is insomnia!

8. **Try counting sheep.** It works! Anything that requires visualization and using the logic center of your brain can help to induce sleep. **Visualize anything you like and count.**

    o Another option is to pay close attention to your breath and count.

Count each exhalation. You might start at 1,000 and count backwards. See how far you can get until your mind wanders away. Return to where you left off and keep counting.

Sleep isn't the most exciting topic, and it might seem too passive to help you deal with the stressors in your life. **However, proper sleep makes you more capable physically and emotionally.** You can't think of many things you do better while tired. Get enough sleep to tackle your worries with energy to spare.

"We all have anxiety about things. We all have little insecurities, but eventually you have to face your fears if you want to be successful, and everybody has some fear of failure."

- Nick Saban

Relaxation Techniques

There are a variety of relaxation techniques you can use to reduce the level of stress in your body. **The best news is that all of these techniques feel incredible.** There are countless options depending on your budget and available time. Enjoy!

Enjoy yourself while relaxing your body and mind with these techniques:

1. **Progressive muscle relaxation.** It's best to do this lying down, but sitting, and even standing, are acceptable. You will start at your feet and move all the way up to your face. You flex and relax each part of your body. When that body part feels relaxed, move to the next.

    - Common areas include: feet, calves, thighs, buttocks, abdominal muscles, hands, forearms, upper arms, shoulders, back, neck and face.

- Really focus on relaxing each body part completely.

2. **Hot tub.** A hot shower or bath can work well, too. Lounge in the warm water and do your best to relax. Combine this technique with progressive relaxation for an even stronger effect.

3. **Massage.** You'll need a few dollars or a friend for this one. If you've never had a massage before, you'll be stunned by how relaxed you feel afterwards. There are many types of massages. Give them all a try.

4. **Sex.** Sex can be a great stress reliever, and it's certainly distracting.

These are just a few ideas to get you started. There are entire industries dedicated to helping you relax and relieve your stress.

Experiment and determine the most effective options for you.

Give your diet, sleep, and exercise a long, hard look. **These things are beneficial to your health as well as dealing with anxiety and worry.** These lifestyle items affect all parts of your life.

"If you believe that feeling bad or worrying long enough will change a past or future event, then you are residing on another planet with a different reality system."

- William James

Chapter 5: Perspective

Stress, worry, and anxiety often have external triggers, but the actual emotions and physical sensations are entirely self-induced. You can't see anxiety. You can only experience it yourself or see other people going through it. It's not growing on a tree or floating through the air.

The way you view life and the challenges you face determines whether or not you'll be anxious when faced with a potential difficulty.

For example, if you think it's important to never feel embarrassed or to make a fool out of yourself, you're going to be more anxious than someone that doesn't hold these beliefs.

Consider how much of a load the average person has put on their brain in order to protect the psyche. They've given it a huge job to do. For example:

- We want to always be happy.
- Of course, we never want to feel embarrassed or psychologically uncomfortable.
- We want everyone to like us.
- We want to ensure we never fail.
- Our brain has to maneuver around every past hurt and concern we've ever had.

Protecting the psyche is a huge job, and it's no wonder why so many people are anxious. A brain that has to deal with all of this can never be 100% emotionally healthy.

"There is nothing that wastes the body like worry, and one who has any faith in God should be ashamed to worry about anything whatsoever."

- Mahatma Gandhi

A healthy perspective on life and challenges can heal anxiety from the inside out.

Consider these ideas:

1. **Remember that life is short.** Imagine you only had a month left to live. How many of your current worries would still bother you? Your perspective changes at the end of your life, but that doesn't mean you can't make changes now.

    - How will you view your life toward the end of your lifetime?

2. **Realize that others aren't really paying attention.** The vast majority of our concerns are regarding the opinions of others. Most of us don't worry about starving to death. We worry about how we look in our old, rusty car.

    - There's good news, though. Few people really care. They're too concerned with other things to be judging. They don't care if you fail or whether you're a few pounds overweight.

- **The people that do care are on your side anyway.**

3. **Understand that few of your worries will actually come true.** You spend a lot of time worrying about things that never happen. One study showed that 85% of worries didn't happen. Of the 15% that did occur, 79% of the study subjects stated the problem was easier to deal with than they expected.

    - A little math (21% of 15%) shows that something "bad" only happens 3.15% of the time when you expect it to happen.

4. **Avoid taking things personally.** So many things are outside of your control, including the attitudes and perceptions of others, that there's no reason to take life personally. If you can remove yourself and your ego

from the equation, there's not much else left to worry about.

5. **Time spent worrying is lost forever.** You don't worry about time when you're younger. At some point, time is all that matters. You're going to kick yourself later for the time you lost to worry. Worrying is akin to taking time and flushing it down the toilet.

Develop a new perspective on life. **You have the right to view the world any way you want.** Create a personal manifesto and live by it. Every person needs a code to follow, or life becomes too complicated.

You might decide that:

- Life is a game full of challenges to solve.

- The purpose of life is spiritual growth.

- You want to learn to be free of the opinions of others.

Create a perspective on life that serves you and either reduces your anxiety or makes good use of it.

"If a problem is fixable, if a situation is such that you can do something about it, then there is no need to worry. If it's not fixable, then there is no help in worrying. There is no benefit in worrying whatsoever."

- Dalai Lama XIV

Chapter 6: Meditation

Everyone talks about mediation these days, but it's been around for thousands of years. **It's a useful tool that many find reduces anxiety and adds enjoyment to their lives.** It's also one of the best ways to learn how your individual brain works.

You learn a lot by sitting still and observing your thoughts and tendencies. **You learn that you are completely separate from your thoughts and urges.** You're just observing them. They don't have to be acted upon.

Meditation quiets the mind and allows you to experience the world free of your opinions and beliefs. **Many proponents of meditation believe that our natural state is one of happiness,** but our perceptions and beliefs are faulty and get in the way of happiness.

While there are meditation retreats, camps, and expert instructors available for hire, you can learn enough on your own to be thrilled with the results. Remember that books and free videos are available, too.

Use meditation as a tool to reduce anxiety and worry, like this:

1. **Find a quiet and comfortable place to sit.** It can be a couch, chair, or pillow on the floor. What's important is that you be comfortable. Staying motionless is important.

    ○ Something firm is more comfortable after a few minutes than something soft.

2. **Start by focusing on your breath.** Just notice and feel the air moving past your nose or lips. Feel your chest expanding and collapsing. Do your best to stay with your breath.

    ○ Eventually, your mind will wander. It might not take long, but the length of time will increase with practice.

3. **Return your attention to your breath for the first week.** For now, just catch yourself when you start daydreaming or thinking about anything other than your breath. Return your focus to the breath.

4. **After a week, stay with the thought for a few minutes.** Observe the thought without engaging with it. You'll know you're doing it wrong if you become emotional in any way. Just notice the thought and sit with it. It will fade on its own if you keep your distance. Then, return to your breath.

5. **Start with five minutes but extend the time to at least 30 minutes.** Meditation is more work than you think. Be gentle with yourself and start slowly. Increase the time over the coming weeks.

That's it! It can be that simple to greatly reduce your anxiety and tendency to worry.

Mastering meditation can take years, but you don't need to be an expert to enjoy great benefits from meditation. Be patient. It's not as easy to sit for 30 minutes as you think.

"Happy is the man who has broken the chains which hurt the mind, and has given up worrying once and for all."

- Ovid

There are several challenges that all meditators face from time to time, including:

1. **Losing focus.** Beginning meditators lose focus easily and don't even realize it until several minutes have passed. We're so used to daydreaming that we fall into that old routine.

    - This is nothing to worry about. Catch yourself as soon in the process as possible and return to your breath.

    - It's challenging to keep your focus for even 30 seconds at first. You have to train your mind to focus for longer. Just keep at it.

2. **Becoming too involved with thoughts.** Your meditation is going well, then you start thinking about your ex and your emotions are off and running. You think about how much you miss him or about how great she used to smell. Next thing you know, you're mad, sad, or lonely.

- View your thoughts like a movie you're not that interested in. They're just things to observe for the time being.

3. **Physical discomfort.** No matter how many times you try, you'll never find a sitting position that's completely pain-free for more than a few minutes. That's okay.

    - Resist the urge to move. The relief you gain is only temporary. You'll just induce a new pain three minutes later.

    - Use your pain as fuel for your meditation. Observe your pain without becoming emotionally involved. In time, it will pass.

4. **Boredom.** Meditation can be boring. Think about just sitting there and watching your breath for an hour. Watching paint dry can be more exciting. Again, just observe your boredom and breathe.

Meditation isn't without its challenges! **You can learn to meditate well enough on your own to experience great results if you're willing to put in the time and effort.**

Meditation has survived for over 3,500 hundred years according to written records.

There's a reason it's still around and more popular than ever.

*"Anxiety is love's greatest killer.
It makes others feel as you might
when a drowning man holds on to you.
You want to save him, but you know he will
strangle you with his panic."*

- Anais Nin

Chapter 7: Mindfulness

A large component of meditation is mindfulness. But you can also be mindful during your regular activities. If you train yourself to be mindful, you'll even be mindful during your dreams.

Mindfulness is simply keeping your awareness on the present moment while accepting any thoughts, emotions, and physical sensations that are present.

In a nutshell, if you're washing the dishes, your mind is on the task of cleaning the dishes. You're also aware of the warmth and wetness of the water. You're not thinking about your bills or the fact that your car is leaking antifreeze.

When you're mindful, you're not overly reactive or bothered by what's happening around you. This isn't because you're unaware, but rather because you're accepting of it. You take on the role of an observer.

You can think of mindfulness as meditating on a task or your environment, rather than allowing your mind to wander off. Can you see how difficult it would be to worry or feel anxiety if you were mindful 100% of the time?

"Anxiety does not empty tomorrow of its sorrows, but only empties today of its strength."

- Charles Spurgeon

Try these ways to be more mindful in your daily life:

1. **Give yourself a reality check by being hyper-aware of your environment.** This is a great way to bring yourself back to the present moment when your mind is running wild. Ask yourself the following questions:

    - What do I see? Describe what you see. For example, "I see a brown, wooden chair with a black padded seat. It has a design of a flower on the back. Describe at least five things you see.

    - What do I hear? Repeat the above process with all of these questions:

    - What do I feel?

    - What do I smell?

    - What do I taste?

2. **Sit outside and observe.** See if you can keep your attention on what you experience with your senses, without thinking about anything.

    - You don't need to tell yourself that you see a tree. After all, It's right in front of you. Just observe and keep your mind as quiet as possible.

    - This can be one of the most relaxing things you can do for your mind. It's a great way to take a break and teach yourself to be mindful.

    - This is also an incredibly safe way to drive a car!

3. **Always maintain at least a slight awareness of your breathing.** Think of your attachment to your breath like a thin thread. It's not at the forefront of your attention while you're having a conversation, but it's always there nonetheless.

- What makes your breath so important is the fact that it's always with you. You take it everywhere you go and it's always happening right now. **It's the perfect anchor to the present.**

4. **Keep your thoughts on what you're doing.** Whether you're taking a shower, eating a burger, or taking out the trash, keep your mind on your current activity. Live your life this way and your anxiety will evaporate.

5. **Only think about the future and the past sparingly.** There's little to be gained by thinking about the past or the future.

    - The past is only useful for learning. Once you've gained the lesson to be learned, come back to the present.

    - Thinking about the future is only useful for planning. Plan your lunch, vacation, or life, but return to the present moment when your planning is done.

- Set aside time to think about the past and future. Have an agenda and stick to it.

6. **Notice how your thoughts rise and fall.** No matter how hard you try, your mind will wander. Observe how thoughts drift away without you having to do anything. They're like clouds floating by. It doesn't take long for them to fade.

7. **Try using mindfulness to improve your diet.** How do we cave in to eating unhealthy foods? We first think about eating the food. Then we get emotionally involved with the idea of how great the food tastes and how good it's going to make us feel. The next thing you know, you're charging the pantry like a mindless fool.

- Try this next time: When you catch yourself craving that bag of chips, be a casual observer of the sensations and emotions you're feeling. You might say to yourself, "My mouth is watering, and I'm getting a warm feeling all over my body. I can already taste the saltiness and feel the crunch of the chips."

- Describe it like you're an impartial scientist doing a study. Focus on those thoughts and feelings. They will go away. Now, you can make a better food choice or find something else to do altogether.

8. **Notice when you tend to space out.** It might be chores or answering emails. When does your mind tend to wander? Pay particular attention at those times and stay mindful.

Mindfulness can be applied during any emotionally charged occasion. **When you're angry, sad, or frustrated, you can use**

mindfulness to move beyond those emotions and make good choices.

Mindfulness creates space for making intelligent decisions based on your knowledge and experience. You can't be wise when reacting to a situation with your emotions raging.

It's also a way to soothe your emotions, including worry and anxiety.

"My life has been full of terrible misfortunes most of which never happened."

- Michel de Montaigne

Chapter 8: Managing Anxiety at Work and Other Specific Locations

Most of us spend the vast majority of our time either at work or at home. **While you now know several tools for dealing with anxiety, each environment is unique.** And it's not just at home or work. You might have high levels of anxiety in social situations.

Let's examine how we can tailor your approach to a specific environment.

Use these techniques to customize your anxiety tools to your work environment:

1. **Understand your triggers at work.** It can be particular situations or people. Maybe you're stressed by a messy desk or by speaking with a certain person. Maybe eating lunch in the work cafeteria frazzles your nerves.

- Make a list of the people and situations that cause you stress, anxiety, or worry.

2. **Plan ahead.** If you know the things that upset you, you can make adjustments and ease your mind.

    - If a messy desk is too much to handle, clean and organize your desk at the end of each day.

    - If a particular person drives you nuts, avoid speaking to them as much as possible. Maybe you can move to a different cubicle or communicate as much as possible via email.

    - Hate the cafeteria scene? Bring your lunch and eat at your desk or get away for an hour.

3. **Have strategies in place for how you will handle any anxiety you do experience.** Maybe you have enough privacy to meditate at work in your

office. Maybe you can hide in the bathroom for a few minutes and meditate.

- You might listen to peaceful music with earbuds.

- You could remember to focus on your breathing.

- You could focus on your surroundings and become as present as possible.

4. **Remind yourself of how much your job does for you.** It allows you to feed yourself and your children, put a roof over your head, and enjoy your life. All of those things can be worth a little aggravation.

Apply these same ideas to the other areas of your life. Work is often the trickiest area because we have the least freedom there. If you can manage work, you should be able to find solutions for the other areas of your life.

- There are more rules regarding your conduct at work than in most other places.

- You don't get to choose all of your coworkers.

- You need a job to survive.

At home, you have more influence over your environment. You also have far more options available to you. Deal with each area of your life individually to maximize the effectiveness of your anti-anxiety strategies.

"A mistake in judgment isn't fatal, but too much anxiety about judgment is."

- Pauline Kael

Chapter 9: Conclusion

Anxiety, worry, stress, and the turmoil they create is damaging to both your physical and emotional health. A plethora of physical ailments are caused or exacerbated by anxiety. **Worrying about the future also detracts from the ability to enjoy life.** It's challenging to enjoy life while in a state of worry.

We often think that worrying is helpful in some way, but it's just a huge waste of energy, time, and happiness.

There are physical and psychological methods of dealing with anxiety and worry. Diet, sleep, exercise, and relaxation techniques can be effective ways to combat anxiety physically.

Psychological techniques include meditation, perspective, and mindfulness. If you find yourself needing additional assistance, there is professional help available. Sometimes coaching, counseling and/or medication are required in more serious cases.

Enjoy your life more by dealing with your anxiety and worry, starting today!

www.ingramcontent.com/pod-product-compliance
Lightning Source LLC
Chambersburg PA
CBHW070542080426
42453CB00029B/954